Discover the Lead

VIOLIN

Classical

Series Editor: Anna Joyce

Editorial, production and recording: Artemis Music Limited • Design and production: Space DPS Limited • Published 2001

IMP

International MUSIC Publications

Introduction

Welcome to DISCOVER THE LEAD, part of an instrumental series that provides beginners of all ages with fun, alternative material to increase their repertoire, but overall, enjoyment of their instrument!

For those of you just starting out, the idea of solo playing may sound rather daunting.
DISCOVER THE LEAD will help you develop reading and playing skills, while increasing your confidence as a soloist.

You will find that the eight well-known songs have been carefully selected and arranged at an easy level - although interesting and musically satisfying. You will also notice that the arrangements can be used along with all the instruments in the series – flute, clarinet, alto saxophone, tenor saxophone, trumpet, violin and piano – making group playing possible!

The professionally recorded backing CD allows you to hear each song in two different ways:

- a complete demonstration performance with solo + backing
- backing only, so you can play along and DISCOVER THE LEAD!

Wherever possible we have simplified the more tricky rhythms and melodies, but if you are in any doubt listen to the complete performance tracks and follow the style of the players. Also, we have kept marks of expression to a minimum, but feel free to experiment with these – but above all, have fun!

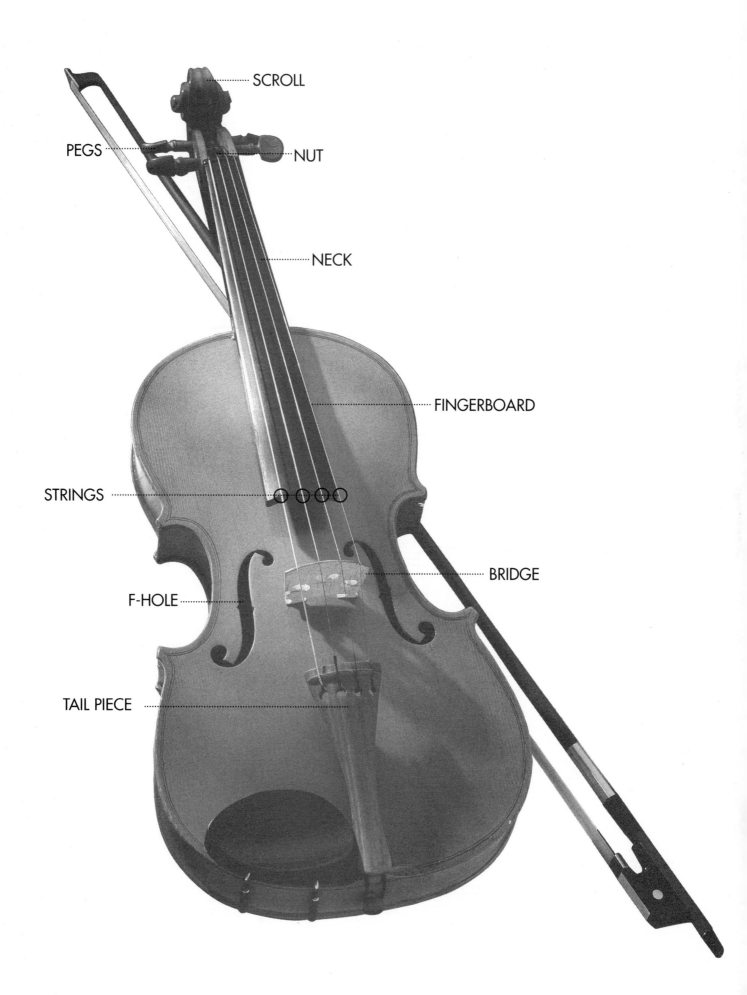

SCROLL

PEGS

NUT

NECK

FINGERBOARD

STRINGS

BRIDGE

F-HOLE

TAIL PIECE

Ave Maria

Music by Franz Schubert

Demonstration   Backing

Demonstration

Backing

La Donna E Mobile
(from *Rigoletto*)

Music by Giuseppe Verdi

Demonstration

Backing

Largo
(from *New World Symphony*)

Music by Antonin Dvořák

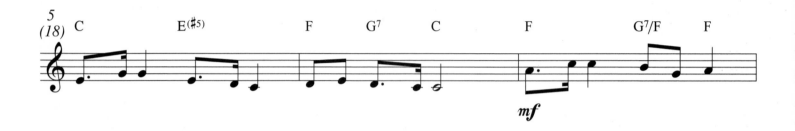

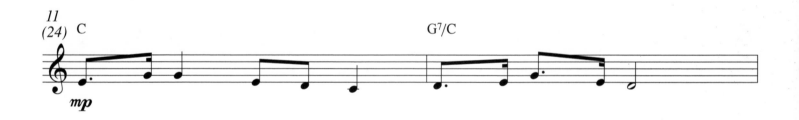

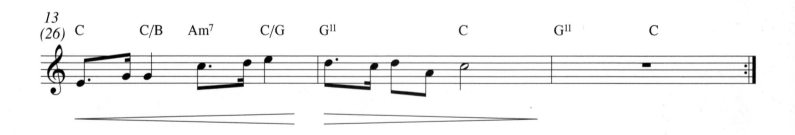

Lullaby
(from *Wiegenlied*)

Music by Johannes Brahms

Demonstration   Backing

Air On A G String

Music by Johann Sebastian Bach

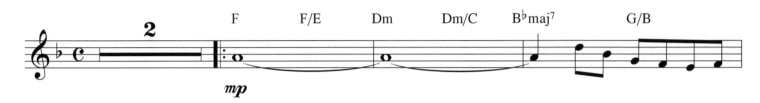

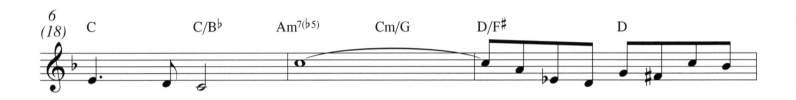

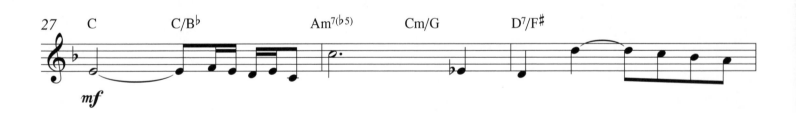

Whatever your instrument is...
you can now

TAKE THE LEAD

- Each book comes with a professionally recorded CD containing full backing tracks for you to play along with, and demonstration tracks to help you learn the songs

- Ideal for solo or ensemble use - in each edition, songs are in the same concert pitch key

- Each book includes carefully selected and edited top line arrangements; chord symbols in concert pitch for use by piano or guitar

- Suitable for intermediate players

"A great way to get some relaxing playing done in between the serious stuff"
Sheet Music Magazine

Discover The Lead

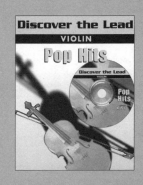

- This new 'spin off' of the Take The Lead series is ideal for beginners of all ages, grades 1-3

- The books contain simplified arrangements of well-known tunes to help the beginner develop reading and playing skills, while increasing confidence as a soloist

- Includes a useful fingering chart plus a CD with full backing and demonstration tracks

- Lots of helpful hints and technical tips to help you get to know your instrument

SHARE THE LEAD

- All pieces have been carefully selected and arranged at an easy level to provide fun material for today's instrumentalists

- All the arrangements work not only as duets for one particular instrument, but with all other instruments in the series (i.e. the flute book works with the clarinet book)

- The professionally recorded CD allows you to hear each song in 4 different ways – a complete demonstration of the track; part two plus backing so you can play along on part one; part one plus backing so you can play along on part two; and the backing only so you and a friend can Share The Lead!

A

Air That I Breathe, The	TTL	- 90s Hits
Air On A G String (Bach)	DTL	- Classical Collection
All Through The Night	TTL	- British Isles Folk Songs
Amazed	TTL	- Ballads
Angels	TTL	- 90s Hits
Ave Maria (Schubert)	DTL	- Classical Collection

B

Bailamos	TTL	- Latin
Be-Bop-A-Lula	TTL	- Rock 'n' Roll
Beautiful Stranger	STL	- Film & TV Hits
Because You Loved Me	TTL	- Movie Hits
Believe	TTL	- Number One Hits
Birdland	TTL	- Jazz
Blue Monday	TTL	- Movie Hits
Blue Suede Shoes	TTL	- Rock 'n' Roll
Blueberry Hill	TTL	- Rock 'n' Roll

C

Careless Whisper	TTL	- Number One Hits
Charlie's Angels	STL	- Film & TV Hits
Chattanooga Choo Choo	TTL	- Swing
Cherry Pink And Apple Blossom White	TTL	- Latin
Choo Choo Ch'Boogie	TTL	- Swing
C'mon Everybody	TTL	- Rock 'n' Roll
Coronation Street	TTL	- TV Themes
Christmas Song, The (Chestnuts Roasting On An Open Fire)	TTL	- Christmas Songs

D

Dance Of The Sugar Plum... The Nutcracker (Tchaikovsky)	TTL	- Classical Collection
Dancing Queen	TTL	- Number One Hits
	STL	- Chart Hits
Desafinado	TTL	- Jazz
Don't Get Around Much Anymore	TTL	- Jazz
Don't Say You Love Me	STL	- Film & TV Hits
Don't Tell Me	DTL	- Pop Hits

E

Everybody Needs Somebody To Love	TTL	- The Blues Brothers
(Everything I Do) I Do It For You	TTL	- Movie Hits

F

Fascinating Rhythm	TTL	- Jazz
Flying Without Wings	TTL	- Number One Hits
	STL	- Chart Hits
Frosty The Snowman	TTL	- Christmas Songs
Frozen	TTL	- 90s Hits

G

Genie In A Bottle	DTL	- Pop Hits
Get Here	TTL	- Ballads
Gimme Some Lovin'	TTL	- The Blues Brothers
Great Balls Of Fire	TTL	- Rock 'n' Roll
Green Door, The	TTL	- Rock 'n' Roll
Greensleeves	TTL	- British Isles Folk Songs
Guantanamera	TTL	- Latin

H

Hall Of The Mountain King from Peer Gynt (Grieg)	TTL	- Classical Collection
Have Yourself A Merry Little Christmas	TTL	- Christmas Songs
Holler	DTL	- Pop Hits
How Do I Live	TTL	- 90s Hits
	STL	- Chart Hits

I

I Believe	STL	- Film & TV Hits
I Don't Want To Miss A Thing	TTL	- 90s Hits
	TTL	- Movie Hits
	TTL	- Ballads
I Will Always Love You	TTL	- Movie Hits
	TTL	- Number One Hits
I'll Be There For You (Theme from Friends)	TTL	- 90s Hits
	TTL	- TV Themes
	STL	- Film & TV Hits
I've Got A Gal In Kalamazoo	TTL	- Swing
In The Mood	TTL	- Swing
It Don't Mean A Thing (If It Ain't Got That Swing)	TTL	- Swing

J

Jailhouse Rock	TTL	- Rock 'n' Roll
Jersey Bounce	TTL	- Swing

L

La Bamba	TTL	- Latin
La Donna E Mobile From Rigoletto (Verdi)	DTL	- Classical Collection
La Isla Bonita	TTL	- Latin
Largo From New World Symphony (Dvorak)	DTL	- Classical Collection

L cont.

Leaving Of Liverpool, The	TTL	- British Isles Folk Songs
Let's Twist Again	TTL	- Rock 'n' Roll
Life Is A Rollercoaster	DTL	- Pop Hits
Little Bit More, A	TTL	- Ballads
Little Donkey	TTL	- Christmas Songs
Livin' La Vida Loca	TTL	- Number One Hits
	TTL	- Latin
Loch Lomond	TTL	- British Isles Folk Songs
Love's Got A Hold On My Heart	STL	- Chart Hits
Lullaby From Wiegenlied (Brahms)	DTL	- Classical Collection

M

Match Of The Day	TTL	- TV Themes
(Meet) The Flintstones	TTL	- TV Themes
Men Behaving Badly	TTL	- TV Themes
Men Of Harlech	TTL	- British Isles Folk Songs
Millennium	DTL	- Pop Hits
Minnie The Moocher	TTL	- The Blues Brothers
Misty	TTL	- Jazz
More Than Words	STL	- Chart Hits
Morning From Peer Gynt (Greig)	DTL	- Classical Collection
My Funny Valentine	TTL	- Jazz
My Heart Will Go On	TTL	- 90s Hits
	TTL	- Ballads
	STL	- Chart Hits

O

Ode To Joy From Symphony No. 9 (Beethoven)	DTL	- Classical Collection
Old Landmark, The	TTL	- The Blues Brothers
One O'Clock Jump	TTL	- Jazz
Oye Mi Canto (Hear My Voice)	TTL	- Latin

P

Peak Practice	TTL	- TV Themes
Pennsylvania 6-5000	TTL	- Swing
Polovtsian Dances from Prince Igor (Borodin)	TTL	- Classical Collection
Pure Shores	STL	- Film & TV Hits

R

Radetzky March (Strauss)	TTL	- Classical Collection
Reach	DTL	- Pop Hits
Rose, The	TTL	- Ballads
Rudolph The Red-Nosed Reindeer	TTL	- Christmas Songs

S

Santa Claus Is Comin' To Town	TTL	- Christmas Songs
Say What You Want	DTL	- Pop Hits
Scarborough Fair	TTL	- British Isles Folk Songs
Searchin' My Soul	STL	- Film & TV Hits
Seasons In The Sun	DTL	- Pop Hits
Shake A Tail Feather	TTL	- The Blues Brothers
She Caught The Katy And Left Me A Mule To Ride	TTL	- The Blues Brothers
Sheep May Safely Graze (Bach)	TTL	- Classical Collection
Simpsons, The	TTL	- TV Themes
Skye Boat Song, The	TTL	- British Isles Folk Songs
Sleigh Ride	TTL	- Christmas Songs
Something About The Way You Look Tonight	TTL	- 90s Hits
Soul Limbo	TTL	- Latin
Spring From The Four Seasons (Vivaldi)	DTL	- Classical Collection
Star Wars (Main Theme)	TTL	- Movie Hits
String Of Pearls, A	TTL	- Swing
Summertime	TTL	- Jazz
Swan, The from Carnival of the Animals (Saint-Säens)	TTL	- Classical Collection
Swear It Again	TTL	- Ballads
Sweet Home Chicago	TTL	- The Blues Brothers
Symphony No. 40 in G Minor, 1st Movement (Mozart)	TTL	- Classical Collection

T

Think	TTL	- The Blues Brothers
Toreador's Song, The from Carmen (Bizet)	TTL	- Classical Collection

W

When Irish Eyes Are Smiling	TTL	- British Isles Folk Songs
When You Say Nothing At All	TTL	- Number One Hits
	STL	- Chart Hits
	STL	- Film & TV Hits
Wind Beneath My Wings, The	TTL	- Movie Hits
	TTL	- Ballads
Winter Wonderland	TTL	- Christmas Songs

X

X-Files, The	TTL	- TV Themes

Y

You Needed Me	TTL	- Number One Hits
	STL	- Chart Hits
You Can Leave Your Hat On	TTL	- Movie Hits

Here's what you get with each book...

Take The Lead

90s Hits
Air That I Breathe - I'll Be There For You - Something About The Way You Look Tonight - Frozen - How Do I Live - Angels - My Heart Will Go On - I Don't Want To Miss A Thing

Movie Hits
Because You Loved Me, Blue Monday, (Everything I Do) I Do It For You, I Don't Want To Miss A Thing, I Will Always Love You, Star Wars, The Wind Beneath My Wings

TV Themes
Coronation Street, I'll Be There For You (Theme from Friends), Match Of The Day, (Meet) The Flintstones, Men Behaving Badly, Peak Practice, The Simpsons, The X-Files

The Blues Brothers
She Caught The Katy And Left Me A Mule To Ride - Gimme Some Lovin' - Shake A Tail Feather - Everybody Needs Somebody To Love - The Old Landmark - Think - Minnie The Moocher - Sweet Home Chicago

Christmas Songs
Winter Wonderland - Little Donkey - Frosty The Snowman - Rudolph The Red Nosed Reindeer - Christmas Song (Chestnuts Roasting On An Open Fire) - Have Yourself A Merry Little Christmas - Santa Claus Is Comin' To Town - Sleigh Ride

Swing
Chattanooga Choo Choo - Choo Choo Ch'Boogie - I've Got A Gal In Kalamazoo - In The Mood - It Don't Mean A Thing (If It Ain't Got That Swing) - Jersey Bounce - Pennsylvania 6-5000 - A String Of Pearls

Jazz
Birdland - Desafinado - Don't Get Around Much Anymore - Fascinating Rhythm - Misty - My Funny Valentine - One O'Clock Jump - Summertime

Latin
Bailamos - Cherry Pink And Apple Blossom White - Desafinado - Guantanamera - La Bamba - La Isla Bonita - Oye Mi Canto (Hear My Voice) - Soul Limbo

Number One Hits
Believe, Cher - Careless Whisper, George Michael - Dancing Queen, Abba - Flying Without Wings, Westlife - I Will Always Love You, Whitney Houston - Livin' La Vida Loca, Ricky Martin - When You Say Nothing At All, Ronan Keating - You Needed Me, Boyzone

Classical Collection
Sheep May Safely Graze (Bach) - Symphony No. 40 in G Minor, 1st Movement (Mozart) - The Toreador's Song from Carmen (Bizet) - Hall Of The Mountain King from Peer Gynt (Grieg) - Radetzky March (Strauss) - Dance Of The Sugar Plum Fairy from The Nutcracker (Tchaikovsky) - Polovtsian Dances from Prince Igor (Borodin) - The Swan from Carnival of the Animals (Saint-Säens)

Rock 'n' Roll
Be-Bop-A-Lula - Blue Suede Shoes - Blueberry Hill - C'mon Everybody - Great Balls Of Fire - The Green Door - Jailhouse Rock - Let's Twist Again

Ballads
Amazed - Get Here - I Don't Want To Miss A Thing - A Little Bit More - My Heart Will Go On - The Rose - Swear It Again - The Wind Beneath My Wings

British Isles Folk Songs
All Through The Night - Greensleeves - The Leaving Of Liverpool - Loch Lomond - Men Of Harlech - Scarborough Fair - The Skye Boat Song - When Irish Eyes Are Smiling

Share The Lead

Chart Hits
Dancing Queen - Flying Without Wings - How Do I Live - Love's Got A Hold On My Heart - My Heart Will Go On - More Than Words - When You Say Nothing At All - You Needed Me

Film & TV Hits
Beautiful Stranger - Charlie's Angels - Don't Say You Love Me - I Believe - I'll Be There For You - Pure Shores - Searchin' My Soul - When You Say Nothing At All

Discover The Lead

Pop Hits
Don't Tell Me - Genie In A Bottle - Holler - Life Is A Rollercoaster - Millennium - Reach - Say What You Want - Seasons In The Sun

Classical Collection
Air On A G String (Bach) - Ave Maria (Schubert) - La Donna E Mobile from Rigoletto (Verdi) - Largo from New World Symphony (Dvorak) - Lullaby from Wiegenlied (Brahms) - Morning from Peer Gynt (Grieg) - Ode To Joy from Symphony No. 9 (Beethoven) - Spring from The Four Seasons (Vivaldi)

Whatever your instrument is...
you can now
TAKE, DISCOVER & SHARE

Available for Violin

7240A	TTL Swing
7177A	TTL Jazz
7084A	TTL The Blues Brothers
7025A	TTL Christmas Songs
7006A	TTL TV Themes
6912A	TTL Movie Hits
6728A	TTL 90s Hits
7263A	TTL Latin
7313A	TTL Number One Hits
7508A	TTL Classical Collection
7715A	TTL Rock 'n' Roll
8487A	TTL Ballads
9068A	TTL British Isles Folk Songs
7287A	STL Chart Hits
8493A	STL Film & TV Hits
8856A	DTL Pop
9165A	DTL Classical Collection

Available for Clarinet

7173A	TTL Jazz
7236A	TTL Swing
7080A	TTL The Blues Brothers
7023A	TTL Christmas Songs
7004A	TTL TV Themes
6909A	TTL Movie Hits
6726A	TTL 90s Hits
7260A	TTL Latin
7309A	TTL Number One Hits
7505A	TTL Classical Collection
7711A	TTL Rock 'n' Roll
8483A	TTL Ballads
9064A	TTL British Isles Folk Songs
7285A	STL Chart Hits
8491A	STL Film & TV Hits
8852A	DTL Pop
9161A	DTL Classical Collection

Available for Drums

7179A	TTL Jazz
7027A	TTL Christmas Songs

Available for Trumpet

7083A	TTL The Blues Brothers
7239A	TTL Swing
7176A	TTL Jazz
7262A	TTL Latin
7312A	TTL Number One Hits
7503A	TTL Christmas Songs
7507A	TTL Classical Collection
7714A	TTL Rock 'n' Roll
8486A	TTL Ballads
9067A	TTL British Isles Folk Songs
8494A	STL Film & TV Hits
8855A	DTL Pop
9164A	DTL Classical Collection

Available for Tenor Saxophone

6911A	TTL Movie Hits
7238A	TTL Swing
7175A	TTL Jazz
7082A	TTL The Blues Brothers
7311A	TTL Number One Hits
7637A	TTL Christmas Songs
7713A	TTL Rock 'n' Roll
8485A	TTL Ballads
9066A	TTL British Isles Folk Songs
9163A	DTL Classical Collection
8854A	DTL Pop

Available for Piano

7178A	TTL Jazz
7026A	TTL Christmas Songs
7364A	TTL Latin
7441A	TTL Number One Hits
7509A	TTL Classical Collection
7716A	TTL Rock 'n' Roll
8488A	TTL Ballads
9069A	TTL British Isles Folk Songs
8857A	DTL Pop
9166A	DTL Classical Collection

Available for Flute

6725A	TTL 90s Hits
7079A	TTL The Blues Brothers
7235A	TTL Swing
7172A	TTL Jazz
7022A	TTL Christmas Songs
7003A	TTL TV Themes
6908A	TTL Movie Hits
7259A	TTL Latin
7310A	TTL Number One Hits
7504A	TTL Classical Collection
7710A	TTL Rock 'n' Roll
8482A	TTL Ballads
9063A	TTL British Isles Folk Songs
7284A	STL Chart Hits
8490A	STL Film & TV Hits
8851A	DTL Pop
9160A	DTL Classical Collection

Available for Alto Saxophone

7005A	TTL TV Themes
7237A	TTL Swing
7174A	TTL Jazz
7081A	TTL The Blues Brothers
7024A	TTL Christmas Songs
6910A	TTL Movie Hits
6727A	TTL 90s Hits
7261A	TTL Latin
7308A	TTL Number One Hits
7506A	TTL Classical Collection
7712A	TTL Rock 'n' Roll
8484A	TTL Ballads
9065A	TTL British Isles Folk Songs
7286A	STL Chart Hits
8492A	STL Film & TV Hits
8853A	DTL Pop
9162A	DTL Classical Collection

Available from:

TTL03

Published by:

IMP

International
MUSIC
Publications

International Music Publications Ltd
Griffin House
161 Hammersmith Road
London
England W6 8BS

Registered In England No. 2703274
A Warner Music Group Company

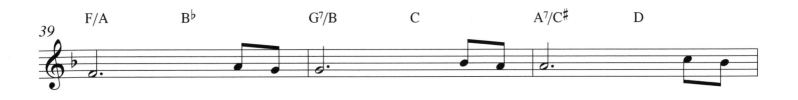

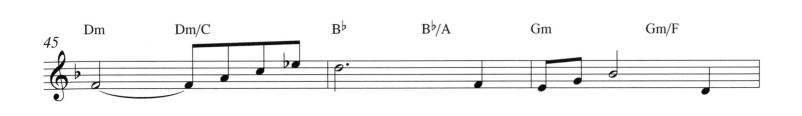

Demonstration

Backing

Morning
(from *Peer Gynt*)

Music by Edvard Grieg

Waltz

mp (1st time)

mf (2nd time)

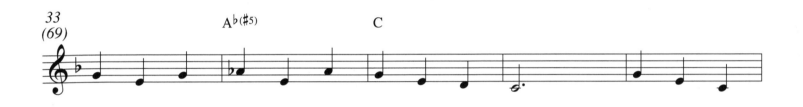

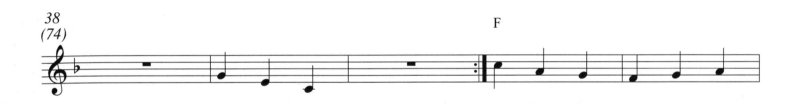

Demonstration   Backing

Ode To Joy
(from *Symphony No. 9*)

Music by Ludwig Van Beethoven

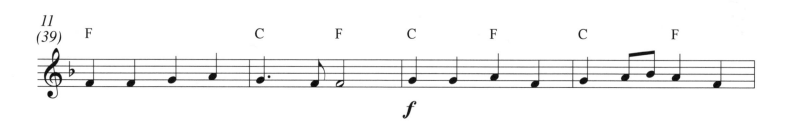

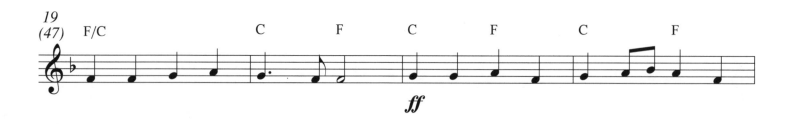

Spring
(from *The Four Seasons*)

Music by Antonio Vivaldi

Demonstration

Backing

Printed in England by Halstan & Co. Ltd., Amersham, Bucks.

A Guide to Notation

Note and Rest Values

This chart shows the most commonly used note values and rests.

Name of note (UK)	Semibreve	Minim	Crotchet	Quaver	Semiquaver
Name of note (USA)	Whole note	Half note	Quarter note	Eighth note	Sixteenth note
Note symbol					
Rest symbol					
Value per beats	4	2	1	1/2	1/4

Repeat Bars

When you come to a double dotted bar, you should repeat the music between the beginning of the piece and the repeat mark.

When you come to a repeat bar you should play again the music that is between the two dotted bars.

First, second and third endings

The first time through you should play the first ending until you see the repeat bar. Play the music again and skip the first time ending to play the second time ending, and so on.

D.C. (Da Capo)

When you come to this sign you should return to the beginning of the piece.

D.C. al Fine

When this sign appears, go back to the beginning and play through to the *Fine* ending marked. When playing a *D.C. al Fine*, you should ignore all repeat bars and first time endings.

D.S. (Dal Segno)

Go back to the 𝄋 sign.

D.S. al Fine

Go to the sign 𝄋 and play the ending labelled *(Fine)*.

D.S. al Coda

Repeat the music from the 𝄋 sign until the ⊕ or *To Coda* signs, and then go to the coda sign. Again, when playing through a *D. 𝄋 al Coda*, ignore all repeats and don't play the first time ending.

Accidentals

Flat ♭ - When a note has a flat sign before it, it should be played a semi tone lower.

Sharp ♯ - When a note has a sharp sign before it, it should be played a semi tone higher.

Natural ♮ - When a note has a natural sign before it, it usually indicates that a previous flat or sharp has been cancelled and that it should be played at it's actual pitch.

Bar Numbers

Bar numbers are used as a method of identification, usually as a point of reference in rehearsal. A bar may have more than one number if it is repeated within a piece.

Pause Sign

A pause is most commonly used to indicate that a note/chord should be extended in length at the player's discretion. It may also indicate a period of silence or the end of a piece.

Dynamic Markings

Dynamic markings show the volume at which certain notes or passages of music should be played. For example

pp	= very quiet	*mf*	= moderately loud
p	= quiet	*f*	= loud
mp	= moderately quiet	*ff*	= very loud

Time Signatures

Time signatures indicate the value of the notes and the number of beats in each bar.

The top number shows the number of beats in the bar and the bottom number shows the value of the note.